What's It About Alphy?

The Christian In Days of Challenge

Alphy the WOW Church Cat Investigates Romans 8

Davo Roberts

Acknowledgements

What's It All About Alphy? The Christian in Days of Challenge – version 1.0

Editing & Proofing: Roger Kirby

Text & Graphics Copyright © 2021 Dave G Roberts

ISBN-13: 9781793448699

Also available in full colour on Kindle.

Dedication

Firstly, to the Lord our God – Father, Son and Holy Spirit. I wouldn't be here without him.

Secondly to my wife, Youngmi. She is my one and my only. I can't imagine life without her. I thank God for her daily.

To the unseen millions who have downloaded Podcasts and watched videos – thanks be to God for you and I hope that each podcast or video, has been of some spiritual help and that God has been glorified.

How To Look Up The Bible

The following diagram will help you if you are not used to reading the Bible.

Contents

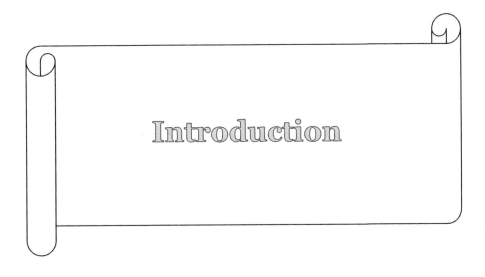

Introduction

Have you ever experienced challenges in your life or witnessed them in the life of somebody else? By challenge, I mean a stimulating or provoking circumstance, trouble, or problem.

If you have not, then you are unique amongst all people of all time! People face challenges face day in and day out. You may well be going through one or more of them yourself now, or you may know of somebody who is.

Let's start by having a look together now at some suggested challenges before we go into the majestic piece of writing that is in Romans 8. Let's have some fun! Can you guess what they are? Answers can be found on page 135.

Challenge 1.

Challenge 2.

Challenge 3.

Challenge 4.

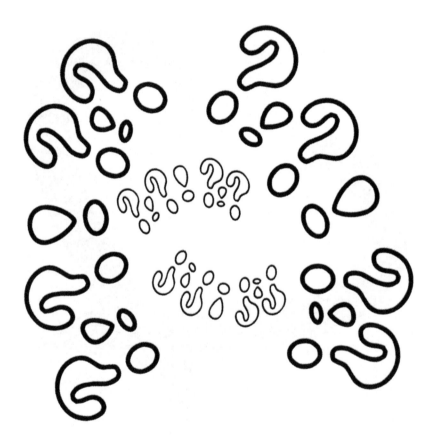

Challenge 5.

Challenge 6.

Challenge 7.

Challenge 8.

Challenge 9.

Challenge 10.

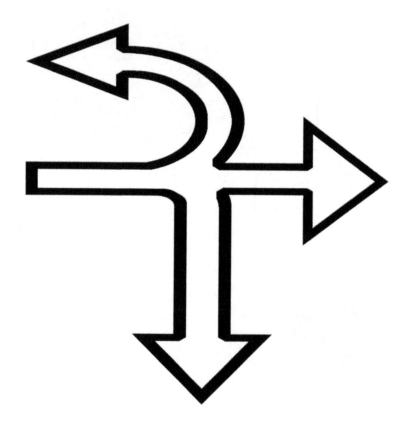

Challenge 11.

Challenge 12.

Challenge 13.

Challenge 14.

Challenge 15.

Challenge 16.

Challenge 17.

Challenge 18.

Challenge 19.

Challenge 20.

With all that looked at, lets now see how we as Christians can overcome these challenges with a look at that majestic piece of literature we know as Romans 8. Are you ready? Come on in!

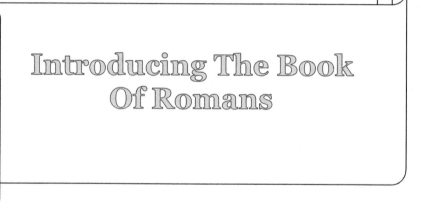

Introducing The Book Of Romans

Let's start by briefly looking at what the book of Romans is all about, before we concentrate on Romans 8.

Paul's letter to the Romans explains what God has done, presenting God's plan of salvation, which is in Jesus Christ, and the effect this has upon all humanity.

This gospel plan sees God's righteousness extended to all of humanity based on Jesus Christ' work on the cross alone. It is received by faith in Him, rather than the good works of man. It investigates ideas such as guilt, faith, assurance, security, and sanctification.

Here are some suggested key verses to the book of Romans:

16 For I am not ashamed of the gospel, because it is the power of God that brings salvation to everyone who believes: first to the Jew, then to the Gentile. 17 For in the gospel the righteousness of God is revealed – a righteousness that is by faith from first to last, just as it is written: 'The righteous will live by faith.' (Romans 1:16-17)

There is no difference between Jew and Gentile, 23 for all have sinned and fall short of the glory of God, 24 and all are justified freely by his grace through the redemption that came by Christ Jesus. (Romans 3:22-24)

Overall, Romans is a book of freedom as it explores how people can be truly free within a dynamic, personal, and intimate relationship with God. With that said, let's see that together now in Romans 8!

Each of us have troubles and suffering which include those which physical, emotional, mental, or spiritual. Regardless of who we are and what social status we hold. Christians are no different. We may have troubles because of the actions of others, or indeed as a result of our own actions or inaction.

Part 1:
Challenge Accepted
(Romans 8:18-30)

¹⁸ I consider that our present sufferings are not worth comparing with the glory that will be revealed in us. ¹⁹ For the creation waits in eager expectation for the children of God to be revealed. ²⁰ For the creation was subjected to frustration, not by its own choice, but by the will of the one who subjected it, in hope ²¹ that the creation itself will be liberated from its bondage to decay and brought into the freedom and glory of the children of God. ²² We know that the whole creation has been groaning as in the pains of childbirth right up to the present time. ²³ Not only so, but we ourselves, who have the first fruits of the Spirit, groan inwardly as we wait eagerly for our adoption to sonship, the redemption of our bodies. ²⁴ For in this hope we were saved. But hope that is seen is no hope at all. Who hopes for what they already have? ²⁵ But if we hope for what we do not yet have, we wait for it patiently.

(Romans 8:18-25)

²⁶ In the same way, the Spirit helps us in our weakness. We do not know what we ought to pray for, but the Spirit himself intercedes for us through wordless groans. ²⁷ And he who searches our hearts knows the mind of the Spirit, because the Spirit intercedes for God's people in accordance with the will of God. ²⁸ And we know that in all things God works for the good of those who love him, who have been called according to his purpose. ²⁹ For those God foreknew he also predestined to be conformed to the image of his Son, that he might be the firstborn among many brothers and sisters. ³⁰ And those he predestined, he also called; those he called, he also justified; those he justified, he also glorified.

(Romans 8:26-30)

In the Bible, all roads seemingly lead to this book of Romans. Paul, here in Romans 5 to 8, is giving glimpses from different angles of how the Christian should live under and within grace – God's unmerited favour to undeserving sinners.

It's as if Paul is creating a fabulous stained glass sphere depicting life for the Christian believer who is now under grace and has Jesus as their master and Lord.

We live in a troubled world, I am sure you are aware, as did the original recipients of Paul's letter. Now Paul is assuring his Roman readers that even when the troubles and sufferings of life hit them, their life in God is secure and their salvation is assured.

An assurance despite what anybody can do to them or what troubles and difficulties they may have to endure.

Paul is assuring them that God will not separate Himself from them during the pains and trials of life. I wonder what you are undergoing currently in your life.

^{18} I consider that our present sufferings are not worth comparing with the glory that will be revealed in us. ^{19} For the creation waits in eager expectation for the children of God to be revealed.
^{20} For the creation was subjected to frustration, not by its own choice, but by the will of the one who subjected it, in hope ^{21} that the creation itself will be liberated from its bondage to decay and brought into the freedom and glory of the children of God.
^{22} We know that the whole creation has been groaning as in the pains of childbirth right up to the present time.

(Romans 8:18-22)

When God finished His creation, it was a good creation. Just as Adam was made in the image of God, so are we. But because of Adam's sin, this imperfect world, including us, bears the mark of sin.

The creation is fallen & marred as are all humans. Creation is groaning. There is suffering and death; there is pain, all of which is, of course, the result of Adam's sin. It is not the fault of creation but of human beings.

²³ Not only so, but we ourselves, who have the first fruits of the Spirit, groan inwardly as we wait eagerly for our adoption to sonship, the redemption of our bodies. ²⁴ For in this hope we were saved. But hope that is seen is no hope at all. Who hopes for what they already have? ²⁵ But if we hope for what we do not yet have, we wait for it patiently.

(Romans 8:23-25)

The creation groans as do we. The reason we as Christians groan, writes Paul, is because we have experienced what he calls "the first-fruits of the Spirit." That is a foretaste of the glory to come when we shall live with Jesus, our King, in glory.

Just as the nation of Israel tasted the first fruits of Canaan when the spies returned (Numbers 12:23-27), so we Christians have tasted the first blessings of heaven through the Holy Spirit's ministry!

This should encourage us to want to see the Lord, receive our new body to live with Him and serve Him forever in everlasting life.

We are waiting for "the great adoption," which is the redemption of our bodies when Jesus returns again.

This is the thrilling climax to "the adoption" that took place at our conversion when the "Spirit of adoption" gave us the standing of an adult in the Kingdom of God.

When Jesus returns, we shall enter into our full inheritance. Meanwhile we wait 'in hope' (Romans 8:24).

What hope is this we ask? It is "The blessed hope and the glorious appearing of the great God and our Saviour Jesus Christ" (Titus 2:13). The best is yet to come! Mee-WOW!

As Christians, people of the Kingdom of God, as God's children, we should not get frustrated as we see and experience suffering and pain in this world. We are people of two passports, one for the land we live in and another for the Kingdom.

Life in the first of those may be tough, but we have another life in the greater, better Kingdom of which Jesus is the King. As we live in the Kingdom, Paul reminds us that Christian believers should know and remember that the suffering of today, will one day give way to eternal glory.

26 In the same way, the Spirit helps us in our weakness. We do not know what we ought to pray for, but the Spirit himself intercedes for us through wordless groans. 27 And he who searches our hearts knows the mind of the Spirit, because the Spirit intercedes for God's people in accordance with the will of God. 28 And we know that in all things God works for the good of those who love him, who have been called according to his purpose. 29 For those God foreknew he also predestined to be conformed to the image of his Son, that he might be the firstborn among many brothers and sisters. 30 And those he predestined, he also called; those he called, he also justified; those he justified, he also glorified.

(Romans 8:26-30)

So, creation groans. God's Kingdom people groan. What about God? Is He an impersonal and distant God who is not concerned with the sufferings of His creation or His people? By no means.

Our God is not a distant God, but a God actively concerned for His creation and for His people. He groans in the person of the Holy Spirit. God is concerned about the sufferings we go through and the troubles we endure. He desires the redemption of His creation and His people.

When Jesus walked the earth, He saw what sin was doing to men, women, and creation (Mark 7:34; John 11:33-38) and this happened. Jesus wept. Isn't that profound?

Paul writes that God the Holy Spirit groans with us and that He feels the burdens of our weaknesses and suffering. What does He do? He responds by lifting us up because He is the Holy Comforter, Counsellor and Helper who lives within us.

As we struggle to persevere, and we sometimes do struggle, is it because we forget to ask for His help, His comfort, and His wisdom? But the Spirit does more than groan: He prays for us in His groaning so that we might be led into the will of God.

We do not always know God's will. We do not always know how to pray, but the Spirit intercedes for us so that we might live in the will of God even though we are suffering in some way. The Holy Spirit shares the burden with us as we endure and persevere.

The phrase "For your good" is a recurring theme throughout the Old Testament. Just a few examples show this to be evident.

Joseph after he is reunited with his brothers said this: You intended to harm me, but God intended it for good (Genesis 50:20)

Moses as he tried to get Israel into shape, while they whinged and whined about the Law frequently told them it was for their own good.

"And now, Israel, what does the LORD your God ask of you but to fear the LORD your God, to walk in obedience to him, to love him, to serve the LORD your God with all your heart and with all your soul, and to observe the LORD's commands and decrees that I am giving you today for your own good?" (Deuteronomy 10:12-13)

Or take Jeremiah, as the ancient Israelites were in exile:

"For I know the plans I have for you,' declares the LORD, 'plans to prosper you and not to harm you, plans to give you hope and a future." (Jeremiah 29:11)

Millions of Christians over the centuries have taken great comfort and hope from Romans 8:28.

I wonder if any of the recipients of this letter, recalled Paul's words to them when the Emperor Nero butchered the Christians in Rome just a few short years later. I imagine that the original readers of this letter to the Romans were greatly comforted.

Paul writes encouragingly here in Romans 8, that "In all things God works for our good." Now the phrase, "all things" includes not only the good, the happy and the pleasant things in life, but also the bad, the unhappy and the unpleasant things as well.

That includes evil, sickness and death. At the times when we are happy and things are going well, it is very easy to agree with this verse. But in times of trouble, this verse is hard to understand and harder still to believe.

We are to recognize too that we don't get to define the 'good'. God does that, and His definition may not be the same as ours would have been! For the millions of Christians who have spent their lives in jail, or have been killed for the faith, we cannot possibly say that all things have been for their good in this world. If that is so, how then are we to understand this verse?

Perhaps we should understand it this way. All the things that happen to us here on earth, God will work for our good in heaven. In the previous verses, Paul teaches about our future hope and future glory. Therefore, in this verse the good that Paul talks about here, is heavenly good, not earthly good.

Having said that it is also true that God is concerned for our welfare in this earthly life. He cares about our bodies, our health, even our food and clothing. When God allows trouble to come into our lives, He usually uses that trouble to bring about some good result in our lives here on earth according to both our writer, Paul and to the Apostle James (Romans 5:3-4; James 1:2-4).

It is through troubles that our faith is tested and strengthened (1 Peter 1:6-7). Through various kinds of trouble God disciplines us, so that we might become more like His Son, Jesus Christ, according to the writer of the book of Hebrews (Hebrews 12:7-11).

The most important thing to remember about this verse, however, is that the promise given here is only applicable to those who love God - those who are his children and in His kingdom. That is those have been called according to His purpose and are therefore members of the kingdom of God.

If we love God, called according to His purpose, and therefore members of the Kingdom of God, then we can fully trust Him to work for our good in all things. Our hope is in God; He is faithful and able to fulfil all He has promised.

As those who are in the Kingdom of God, that is all believing Christians, Paul exhorts us to never give up in times of trial and suffering because God is at work in the world (Romans 8:28). Paul encourages us that God has a supreme plan (Romans 8:29) and that He has two purposes in that plan: His glory alone and our good.

Ultimately, Christians will be transformed into the likeness of the Lord Jesus Christ – that is God's ultimate goal for us: to be like His Son. Best of all, God's plan will succeed – He has the victory, and that victory was gained at the Cross of Jesus at Calvary.

It started in eternity when He chose us in Jesus Christ. God predestined that one day we would be like His Son. The word 'predestined' here applies only to those in the Kingdom of God, not to those outside the Kingdom. Nowhere in Scripture are we taught that God chooses who will remain outside the kingdom.

If people remain outside the kingdom, it is because they choose to do so, by refusing to trust and believe in Jesus Christ. Those whom He chose, God called (2 Thessalonians 2:13-14). When they responded to His call, He justified them by taking away their guilt and sin, and He also glorified them.

This means that the believer has already been glorified in Jesus (John 17:22); the revelation of that glory awaits the coming of the Lord Jesus Christ.

So far, we have seen together that God is not distant but is close and personal and that we know He Himself has suffered. He cares for His creation and for His people through the ministry of God the Holy Spirit.

Times of trouble may come, but even through them, we are being transformed into the image of God the Son, Jesus Christ. We have seen that we will one day have freedom from pain and suffering. Freedom to live properly. We also saw that we need not fear separation from God because the relationship between God and the Christian is utterly assured! Why? Jesus' death and resurrection!

God is for us. Christ died for us. God the Holy Spirit lives within us, praying for us, guiding us, and empowering us. He is the seal of our salvation. We are declared God's sons and daughters if we choose to follow Him. Jesus Christ prays for us and He loves us.

Do you get discouraged and frustrated in times of trouble as I do sometimes? I have to ask myself questions. Questions such as how can we believers ever be discouraged and frustrated when we already share the glory of God?

Our suffering today, guarantees much glory for us, when Jesus Christ Himself returns in glory. How can we be discouraged when the God we love and serve, who has called us to follow Him, Himself had great anxiety the night before He suffered and died on the Cross, but was faithful to the end?

How can we be discouraged, when we know that this Jesus rose from the dead and ascended back to the Father? Jesus still had his scars when he ascended.

How can we be discouraged when we know that Jesus will come back again one day to gather us for Himself?

Where is God? What does He have to do with our lives? God does not shelter us from the sufferings and hard times of life because we need them for our spiritual growth (Romans 5:3-5) and for our transformation into the image of Jesus, God's Son.

We know that God assures us that the difficulties of life are working for us and not against us (Romans 8:28). God allows trials and sufferings to come that they may be used for our good and His glory.

We endure trials for His sake (Romans 8:36), and when we do, do you think that He will abandon us? Of course not. Instead, He lifts us through the hard times.

As we close this part of Romans 8, we know that each person has troubles of some shape or form. There are no easy answers to most of them.

I don't even have answers for my own troubles. My memory some days is like a sieve; a result of that stroke I had. Other days it is more like a funnel.

But I know God is there – I may forget many things, but I have not yet forgotten that. It is God whom I depend upon and personally know to be totally reliable in every way.

For those in the community surrounding us, we Christians need to be God's hands and feet. We need to show people that God radically cares and loves for each of them.

Too often people in need, both within the church and outside it, are shown care and concern for a little while.

But gradually as time goes on, the caring and loving of that person diminishes and ultimately ceases.

Persistent persevering to love and care is required. We can love and care for all using the power and imagination of the Holy Spirit who lives within us.

All sorts of excuses are given for not showing care and love, but in reality, there can be no excuse or reason. Not caring means not loving.

Love is to be shown to all people, regardless of personalities, conflicts, opinions, gender, sexuality, prejudice, and bias. You don't have to agree with people's choices, but you do have to show you love and care for them.

The troubles and suffering we endure, are all part of living in the kingdom of God, part of life.

It is, as we look to the future, that we are being transformed into the image of Jesus and moving towards the supreme glory of God. Not for our own glory however, but for His glory.

In any form of trouble, pain or suffering that we endure, we aren't to give up, but we are to persevere. Why? Because our God perseveres with us because God has not given up on us.

God the Son died on the Cross and rose again from the dead so that you may have new life. WOW!

God the Holy Spirit lives within you. For it is when we are weak, that we are strong – through God. Hold on to Jesus. The Jesus who said, "Come to me all who are burdened and heavy laden and I will give you rest." (Matthew 11:28-30). The Jesus that will one day take our face in His hands and wipe away our tears.

Oh what an amazing day that will be. We will say, it was all worth it. And yet, even though I know this, I still have the impudence to often cry out with frustration and confusion to the Father "why Dad?"

And then He assures me that he loves me with an everlasting and enduring love.

The Church, including you and I as Christians are to go and radically show love and care for all others that we meet or others that we know who need to see God's radical love and care in action.

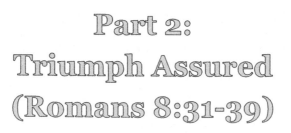

Part 2:
Triumph Assured
(Romans 8:31-39)

31 What, then, shall we say in response to these things? If God is for us, who can be against us? 32 He who did not spare his own Son, but gave him up for us all – how will he not also, along with him, graciously give us all things? 33 Who will bring any charge against those whom God has chosen? It is God who justifies. 34 Who then is the one who condemns? No one. Christ Jesus who died – more than that, who was raised to life – is at the right hand of God and is also interceding for us. 35 Who shall separate us from the love of Christ? Shall trouble or hardship or persecution or famine or nakedness or danger or sword?

(Romans 8:31-35)

36 As it is written:
'For your sake we face death all day long; we are considered as sheep to be slaughtered.'
37 No, in all these things we are more than conquerors through him who loved us. 38 For I am convinced that neither death nor life, neither angels nor demons, neither the present nor the future, nor any powers, 39 neither height nor depth, nor anything else in all creation, will be able to separate us from the love of God that is in Christ Jesus our Lord.

(Romans 8:36-39)

Here in what is quite possibly the most profound section of the Bible, Paul is giving 8 different glimpses from different angles about the Christian living under and within grace – God's unmerited favour to undeserving sinners.

We now go on to this magnificent piece of Scripture before us – Romans 8:31-39.

Of course, Paul is speaking to those having accepted God's free offer of salvation.

Those who have accepted God's invitation of love to enter into relationship with Him through the life, death, and resurrection of Jesus Christ. Would that include you?

Paul starts off with a question "What, then, shall we say in response to this?" By this, he means all that he has said in the first 8 chapters of this magnificent letter. Paul is challenging his readers to question him and fault him.

He asks questions of his readers so that in supplying answers to his own rhetoric, he can tell these Roman believers – and us - that salvation is entirely dependent upon God and nothing will take them - or us - away from God now that a relationship with Him is established.

Is there anything in the universe at all, that can separate you from God and His love for you? Worries? Troubles? War? Condemnation? Doubts? Nothing.

Perhaps God's fickleness? No way. Persecution? Famine? Nakedness? Danger? Sword?

Nothing. Not a chance. Nothing, Paul asserts. Absolutely nothing can separate the Christian from God. And His love for them. WOW! How is this so?

Because the Son of God, Jesus Christ Himself, has justified us before God, intercedes for us before God and more profoundly and deepest of all, He personifies love! He loves us! Jesus loves us. Jesus loves me. Jesus loves you. WOW!

Together, we will relate this magnificent writing not just to Paul's original readers, but also to ourselves some 2,000 years later. Are you ready?

Paul has in mind that when hard times, troubles and suffering come we are strongly tempted to fail to trust in God. We doubt and think that we have been separated from God — we are apart from Him.

In particular, if we are conscious of some failure in our lives it is natural for us to think that somehow we have been separated from the Kingdom as a result. But it is not so.

The emphasis of this section is the security of the believer. The way that once God has us in His grasp, He does not let go. Once the believer is in Christ they do not need to fear the past, present or the future.

Why? Because as God's children they are for ever secure in the love of Jesus. There are 5 reasons why we are secure and will never be separated from God if we belong to the Kingdom.

God is for us (Romans 8:31): we have enemies as Christians. We do have those who are against us. The world and the devil are against us.

But while they are powerful, they are not all-powerful as our God is. And we have God on our side. WOW!

How is this seen? God the Father is for us and has proved it by giving His Son (Romans 8:32). God the Son is for us (Romans 8:34) and so is God the Spirit (Romans 8:26).

Sometimes we are like Jacob and cry "Everything is against me" (Genesis 42:3), when in fact, everything is working for us, for "If God is for us, who can be against us?" (Romans 8:31).

As we enter each day, we should realize that God is for us. There is no need to fear anything, for the loving Father desires only the best for His children, even if they must go through some suffering to receive His best.

For as the prophet Jeremiah, who know his own share of troubles and problems, writes:

'For I know the plans I have for you," declares the Lord, "plans to prosper you and not to harm you, plans to give you hope and a future" (Jeremiah 29:11).

Jesus Christ died for us, exclaims Paul (Romans 8:32): Paul continues to say that if when we were outside the Kingdom of God as non-believers God gave us His best, now that we are His children and within His kingdom, will He not give us all that we need?

Jesus Christ used this same argument when He tried to convince people that it was foolish to worry and fear. God cares for the birds and the sheep, and even for the flowers in the fields; surely He will care for you. God is dealing with His people on the basis of grace, freely giving all things necessary to His people in His Kingdom.

Paul points to the Cross of Jesus Christ. Paul is arguing that just as God gave everything in the costly gift of His Son, Jesus Christ, God will continue to be unfalteringly generous in provided all the needs of those who are His children.

Not only that, but God has justified us before Himself (Romans 8:33) This means that He has declared us right before Himself because of Jesus Christ and we are now members of His kingdom.

Satan would like to accuse us (Zechariah 3:1-7.; Revelation 12:1-10.), but we in the kingdom of God stand firm in Jesus Christ.

We are God's chosen in Jesus Christ and are accepted. God will not accuse us since it is He who has justified us.

For God to accuse us would mean that His salvation was a failure, and we are still in our sins.

We may accuse ourselves, and other people may accuse us, but God will never take us to court and accuse us.

Why is this? Simply, stated because God the Son, Jesus Christ Himself, has already paid the penalty and we are secure in Him. Our salvation is assured because God has His hand in ours. Therefore, who can or will accuse us?

The Devil certainly tries, as that is one of his names – the Accuser. People we know will also accuse us and point a mocking and condemnatory finger at us. But none of their accusations and allegations can be sustained because as Christians we are justified by God before God and for God. Despite the taunts and accusations of others.

Our enemies & detractors not only accuse us, but they also try to condemn us. We even sometimes try to condemn ourselves. But for those in Christ Jesus, those who are believers and call themselves Christian, there is no condemnation before Almighty God.

Why? Because Jesus, the very Son of God Himself, died on the Cross and was raised to new life before He ascended back to God where he does the most extraordinary thing for us. Jesus now prays for us. Is that not simply amazing?

Indeed, both the Holy Spirit and Jesus Christ pray for us (Romans 8:26-27, 34). The same Saviour who died for us is now praying for us in heaven. Jesus is our great Advocate and High Priest. As Jesus is our interceding High Priest, He can give us the grace we need to overcome temptation and defeat the enemy (Hebrews 4:14-16).

As our Advocate, Jesus can forgive our sins and restore our fellowship with God (1 John 1:9-2:2). Intercession means that Jesus Christ represents us before the throne of God, and we do not have to represent ourselves. I still find that amazing, don't you?

Trouble!

Hardship!

Persecution!

Famine (that is lack of food)!

Nakedness (that is lack of clothing)!

Danger or Sword (that is persecution)!

Death nor life!

Angels nor demons!

The present nor the future!

Any powers!

Height nor depth!

nor anything else in all creation!

Christ loves us and because He loves us, Paul goes on to say we are conquerors – overcomers – victors. What are we conquerors of and overcomers over? Look at this list above and be prepared to go WOW! Recognize any of these that you are scared of or in fear of?

None of those things can separate us from the love of God that is in Christ Jesus. Nothing can separate the Christian from God because God lives within them. Because of Jesus, God is for us. God justifies us because of Jesus' death on the Cross. Jesus intercedes for us and Jesus loves us.

The most profound piece of wisdom is that Jesus loves me. Jesus loves you. WOW!

Here in Romans 8:36, Paul refers to Psalm 44:22. Where the Psalmist is complaining about the heavy hand of God being put upon His people without cause and as innocent lambs being slaughtered. There is a remarkable difference in the tone of Paul's writing.

Paul, instead of being downcast, writes rejoicing in persecution and troubles. The Psalmist is complaining, and Paul is rejoicing. What a difference from opposite sides of the Cross of Jesus Christ.

The Psalmist was writing before the coming of the Messiah, Jesus Christ. Paul was writing after Jesus Christ had lived, died, risen to new life, and ascended back to the right-hand side of God.

Paul told his readers, that God cannot fail them, regardless of what life throws at them. Paul explained that nothing could now separate them from the love God in Jesus Christ.

We have seen in our look through Romans, that God does not shelter us from the sufferings and hard times of life. He doesn't do that because we need them for our spiritual growth. (Romans 5:3-5)

As we saw earlier in Romans 8:28, God assures us that the difficulties of life are working for us and not against us. God allows trials and sufferings to come that they may be used for our good and His glory.

We endure trials for His sake (Romans 8:36). Since we do, do you think that He will abandon us? Of course not. Instead, He comes closer to us through the hard times.

God Himself gives us the power to conquer and overcome (Romans 8:37). We are more than conquerors, super-conquerors, for the Lord Jesus Christ. He gives us the victory and adds more victory. When Jesus Christ died on the Cross and rose again three days later, victory was assured.

Victory was won. We need fear neither life nor death, events past, events today or events in the future, because Jesus Christ loves us and gives us the victory.

This is not a promise with conditions attached. It most certainly is not "If you do this, God will do that."

The security that we Christians have in and through Jesus Christ alone is established, and we claim it for ourselves because we are in Jesus Christ.

Have your responded to His claims yet? Nothing can separate us from Jesus Christ, so we should believe it and rejoice in it. Death will not separate the Christian from God — because as soon as the Christian dies physically, they enter God's presence.

It's a complete and blessed assurance. WOW

One other thing we all have had experience of, as well as troubles, is doubt. It is, I think, a very rare person indeed who has not suffered some form of doubt.

By doubt, I do not mean as in doubting God's very existence, but rather doubting some aspect of the Christian life such as the example given here by Paul – the closeness of God.

It is all too easy to think we have been separated from God, either because of something we have done, or our general sense of inferiority to a Holy God.

Paul, with these questions that he poses here in Romans 8, seems to me, to be fervently and emphatically encouraging his readers to remove any doubt in their minds about being separated from God.

Yet even the most ardent and mature of believers have moments of doubt. We all have doubts at times, don't we? Even if we aren't aware of them. When we sin, which we all do at times, we are doubting God. When we fail to do what we ought to do, we are doubting God and His salvation of us.

When we fail to do what we know we ought to do, we are doubting God and His salvation for us. Isn't that when the world taunts us and says "Well you are a fine Christian. Look at what you did."

Our great enemy, satan, accuses the Christian all the time! "Look at what you did, you miserable human. God won't want you anymore. Ha! Ha!" Or is it just me? What can we do with such doubts?

Firstly, there are usually reasons behind why we are doubting.

For instance, when doubt arises concerning God's assured promise of salvation to you, well that usually occurs after we have engaged in wilful sin or have lost a spiritual battle. When we sin, not only do we forget who we are as His children, but we also doubt what God has said is true in the Bible.

With that said, what are some suggested ways in which we can overcome our doubts?

Read and study the Bible, God's Word, so that you get to know, understand, and live truth. Our lives are to be controlled by truth as revealed in Bible. When we know truth really well, we can recognize the lies that we are told.

The Word of God, the Bible, is there to be studied diligently so that by trusting in the Holy Spirit to lead and reveal it to us, we get to know God and His promises.

Then when we hear that nagging little voice that says "God doesn't love you anymore. Haha!" we can say "Oh yes, He does. He died to prove His love of me so that I may truly live for Him."

Confess your doubt to God, and He will listen and cleanse you. If doubts persist, try talking to somebody whom you trust and confess to them your doubts, and they may well be able to help you (James 5:16).

Don't let your thinking and therefore your life be ruled by your emotions. Emotions can go up and down depending on whether you ate a good breakfast or not! Keep your basic thinking firmly anchored to the things of Scripture.

As with your emotions, don't let your thinking be ruled by excitable and excited people who can go up and down depending on whether they ate a good breakfast or not! Keep your basic thinking firmly anchored to that of Scripture.

Exhibit faith in God by showing total trust of Him in your life. Faith is a defensive weapon against the mistruths and doubts that enter our minds. By maintaining our trust in God's promises and God's power, doubts are extinguished.

Read the Bible, God's Word, so that you get to know, understand, and live truth. Our lives are to be controlled by truth as revealed in Bible. When we know truth really well, we can recognize the lies that we are told.

Pray to God. Talk to Him intimately. This is how we are energized. Fighting doubt in our own power is useless. Ask God to help you to overcome doubts, He will help. Our relationship with God grows stronger as we talk openly with Him.

When we see God answer prayer, our faith is matured, and doubts are more easily cast aside. And if struggling in prayer, ask somebody else to pray for you and with you.

Live a righteous life. Live the truth. Live a life which is pleasing to God. When we started the Christian life, we were given the righteousness of Jesus. But that righteousness needs to be lived out in the lives of Christian Disciples. Living right helps overcome any doubts.

Remember that you have assurance of salvation. Be assured and let your mind be controlled by the Holy Spirit, so that you are not led astray. Your salvation rests on nothing apart from God's promises and Jesus' righteousness.

Finally, come back to this passage in Romans 8. Test yourself as Paul exhorts elsewhere (2 Corinthians 13:5). Memorise it if you can. Then be wowed again by the way God helps you and shows you His love of you.

Paul's questions here in Romans 8, tell us about the God we believe in. God loves us. Our confidence is to be in Him and Him alone. His love is always constant and always full on. His great love is not feeble, fickle, or pernickety.

That may well be the way our love for Him is, but it is not how His love for us is. His love for us is always almighty, majestic, preserving, affirming, stable, assuring, true and steadfast. We persevere for God because He perseveres with us.

Then we looked at the ways we can overcome those times of doubt we all have at one time or another. We can overcome by confessing to God, being assured, living a right life worthy of God. We can demonstrate our faith by showing total trust in God for our lives, reading and studying God's Word and talking to Him.

Overall, we can be assured that God, Father, Son and Spirit, is for you, lives within you and nothing, absolutely nothing can separate you from Him because He has you in His hands. He lives within you. WOW!

Know that there is to be no fear of separation from God. God is for you. Christ died for you. God the Holy Spirit lives within you, praying for you, guiding you, empowering you and is the seal of your salvation.

God has put His mark upon you – you are His child, and He loves you.

Jesus Christ exemplified God's love for you, by dying on the Cross for you. Why did He do that? So that you may have new life and live to the full in the splendour and glory of God.

God has declared you to be His son or daughter because you have chosen to follow Him. Jesus Christ prays for you and He loves you.

As a Christian, be assured, go, be a super-conqueror for God in the big outside world. Is that not a great comfort to know? Scripture can be a great comfort. But as I am sure you are aware, while Scripture is meant to be a comfort, it is also meant to be a challenge. Scripture is two-sided.

But as I am sure you are aware, while Scripture is meant to be a comfort, it is also meant to be a challenge. Scripture is two-sided. The challenge for us from this passage of Scripture is two-fold.

Our first challenge is that we are to live such lives as Christians, that when we are accused by satan or other people, the accusations themselves are ridiculed and not us ourselves.

Our second challenge is that we are to tell others about this God of love. We are to tell others that people can enter into a living and dynamic relationship with God only through the death and resurrection of Jesus Christ and Him alone. When was the last time you told somebody this good news of Jesus Christ?

When was the last time you told somebody this good news of Jesus Christ? Ask the Spirit who lives within you, for His assistance and for the opportunities for you to do so. Part of that maybe telling how you have overcome challenges and troubles in your life.

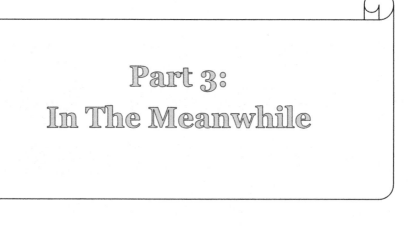

Part 3:
In The Meanwhile

¹⁶ Therefore we do not lose heart. Though outwardly we are wasting away, yet inwardly we are being renewed day by day. ¹⁷ For our light and momentary troubles are achieving for us an eternal glory that far outweighs them all. ¹⁸ So we fix our eyes not on what is seen, but on what is seen is temporary, but what is unseen is eternal.

(2 Corinthians 4:16-18)

Having looked at Romans 8, let's now reinforce what we have seen far but looking more generally at what the Bible has to say, particularly about persevering in our faith.

I wonder if sometimes you feel just like giving up on God, the Church and Christianity. You just want to throw it all away and just be buried by whatever is burdening you. You are feeling deflated, troubled, and overwhelmed.

Almost everyone has felt like that at one time or another. I know that I have. How are you and I to respond to suffering and other troubles?

The ancient prophet Jeremiah certainly did, which even a cursory look at his life story will reveal that to you!

Whatever the challenge is, as a Christian you are to persevere. We persevere because we are not alone in our challenges. Also, if we think about it, in the light of eternity, the time of endurance through these troubles, is but the blink of an eye. WOW!

How are you and I to respond to suffering and other challenges? Naturally, we either treat them too flippantly or far too seriously. The response that God wants His followers to have is to be exercised by it.

When we undergo any challenge, suffering or trouble, we are to commit it to God, endure it and understand that He is faithful and that it will eventuate in His glory and for our own good (Romans 8:28; 1 Peter 4:1). We are to be joyful when enduring suffering (James 1:2).

I admit freely that can be pretty hard to do, but we are not left alone. The Holy Spirit indwells us if we are followers of Jesus. One of His names is that of 'Comforter', because He provides comfort during the difficult times and perseveres in doing so. Just as He perseveres with us, so should we in living for Him.

Perseverance in relation to God and His work is the continuous operation of the Holy Spirit in your life as a believer. It is a work of divine grace that is begun in your heart, which is continued and brought to completion.

As a Christian, you will never perish, and nobody or nothing can snatch them out of His hand (John 10:27-29). You have eternal life, and you will not be condemned by God, having passed from death to life (John 5:24).

God, who began a good work in you, will carry it on to completion (Philippians 1:6). You are shielded by God's power (1 Peter 1:15) and nothing or nobody can ever separate you from God/Christ's love (Romans 8:38-39). God's whole purpose for you is to transform you into the image of His Son, Jesus Christ.

His purpose for you is to make you holy. This is where perseverance for you as a Christian comes in. He may well, as we have seen, use some form of temporal suffering in order to achieve it, but in the light of eternity, it will not be for long.

You are to keep your eyes focussed on Jesus Christ, carry your cross daily and be willing to obey Him. You are to run the race with eyes fixed ahead, forgetting what is past and not looking back at what in the past had entangled us.

And yes that can be hard to forget, but with the help of the Holy Spirit who lives within you, it is possible. As a Christian, persevere in your relationship with God. Obey Him and follow Him.

Ask questions humbly of Him and expect Him to answer, particularly if you don't understand something. Persevere in your prayers, your relationships with God and with other people.

God will persevere with you, turning you gradually into the image of His Son, Jesus Christ. God will not abandon you, but you are free to abandon Him. If you did abandon Him, He would still continue to call you back to Himself. If He perseveres, so must you and me.

But why do we persevere? Character results from persevering. As a Christian you are to be transformed and developed, working on improving your service and being transformed in the image of Jesus Christ. That is God's ultimate purpose for you.

For that to actually occur we need to find out what needs to be developed. These ten characteristics will help you to measure how much the Holy Spirit has been free to develop your character into one that glorifies God alone.

¹⁷ He is before all things, and in him all things hold together. ¹⁸ And he is the head of the body, the church; he is the beginning and the firstborn from among the dead, so that in everything he might have the supremacy.

(Colossians 1:17-18)

Firstly, believe God! What is there in your life that you are trusting in God for that He alone can do (2 Corinthians 4:7)? In your life, Jesus Christ is to be number one and have the complete supremacy and glory over all things in your life.

Whatever you are going through – persevere and develop character. Allow yourself to be transformed daily by God the Holy Spirit into the image of God the Son in obedience to the will of God the Father.

¹¹ I am not saying this because I am in need, for I have learned to be content whatever the circumstances. ¹² I know what it is to be in need, and I know what it is to have plenty. I have learned the secret of being content in any and every situation, whether well fed or hungry, whether living in plenty or in want. ¹³ I can do all this through him who gives me strength.

(Philippians 4:11-13)

While persevering you will grow in confidence - The number one problem in our culture today, is a lack of confidence. For you as a Christian Disciple, self-confidence is to Christ-confidence - this is not egotism.

Say to yourself: "I can't lose. I can only make mistakes". Confidence is spawned by the ability to say no.

The New Testament is the doctrine of moderation in all things. You don't have to do everything you are capable of achieving.

This will in turn lead you to be a consistent example! Modelling is the greatest unconscious form of learning what we know.

The Apostle Paul writes and commands:

"follow me as I follow Christ"

(Philippians 3:17–4:9).

Whether you like it or not, people are following you. However, are you following Christ closely? Those who are following and watching you, in all probability will not do what you tell them to do, but in all likelihood will do what you do. They will copy you.

Persistence and endurance are developing your staying power, to hold on courageously whilst under fire. In other words - bulldog tenacity. Things like criticism, circumstances, opposition & problems can stop you cold if you allow them. The problem is that we sometimes think the Christian life is a sprint race.

When in fact it is a marathon, where a second wind of the long hard grind is necessary. What is it that stops you? The size of a person is determined by what it takes to stop him or her. Winners are people who have formed the habit of doing things that failures hate to do. Don't let anything stop you.

Hold onto having a positive attitude. A danger in becoming negative, is that a root of bitterness sets up. The greatest therapy is that of thanksgiving & prayer. God says you can do it. Satan says you can't do it.

This all helps building up your resistance. Not resistance to ideas but resistance to those who oppose you and your ideas. Criticism is the occupational hazard for leaders. Discouragement is a cancer of the Spirit. Be resistant to discouragement and hyper-criticism. Let the Holy Spirit encourage you.

¹ Therefore, since we are surrounded by such a great cloud of witnesses, let us throw off everything that hinders and the sin that so easily entangles. And let us run with perseverance the race marked out for us, ² fixing our eyes on Jesus, the pioneer and perfecter of faith. For the joy set before him he endured the cross, scorning its shame, and sat down at the right hand of the throne of God.

(Hebrews 12:1-2)

Demonstrate and practise self-mastery and self-control. You need to be unencumbered by the things that weigh you down. This is the danger of an affluent society.. You need to decide what is good and what is evil.

The real decision is between that which is good, that which is better, and which is better or best. Choose the best. We are to travel light, suggests the writer of the letter to the Hebrews, putting off anything that hinders or holds us back. (Hebrews 12:1-2)

²⁵ Jesus called them together and said, 'You know that the rulers of the Gentiles lord it over them, and their high officials exercise authority over them. ²⁶ Not so with you. Instead, whoever wants to become great among you must be your servant, ²⁷ and whoever wants to be first must be your slave – ²⁸ just as the Son of Man did not come to be served, but to serve, and to give his life as a ransom for many.'

(Matthew 20:25-28)

Servanthood is to be shown to all others. The first shall be last and the last shall be first. Priority is to be given to service. An essential part of developing character is serving. If Jesus, as King, could be a humble servant, in that He came to earth as a member of His own creation, then you and I can also be identified as humble servants.

A core part of servanthood is being teachable because we have an unlimited ceiling of being taught. That means having a willingness to be taught by other people, even if you are in a teaching role. The Holy Spirit is the greatest Teacher, so we listen to Him as we are controlled by Him and keeping in step with Him.

Overall, two things to keep in balance are involvement & isolation. You cannot do enough for others if you are constantly in the company of others. You also need time alone but not as a complete hermit shut away from those in your community.

In all these areas, you and I can ask for help from God the Holy Spirit, who lives within us because we are His children.

As Christians, we can confidently ask for Him to assist us to be a consistent example, persistence & endurance, resistance, positive attitude, self-mastery, servanthood, teachability, having a virile private life and a capacity to believe God. When was the last time you asked for His help in these matters?

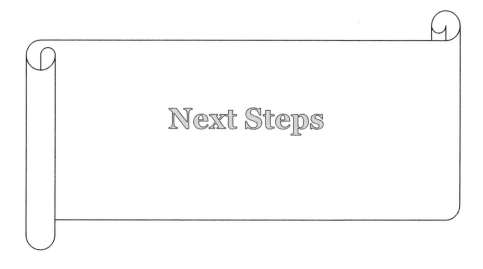

Next Steps

If while you have read this little book, the Holy Spirit has convicted you of your own sin, then you need to confess that sin and repent.

God is love and He loves to forgive those who come to Him in penitence and faith. God is faithful and just and will forgive you from His wellsprings of grace and mercy if you ask for it.

If you want to turn to God right now, and start following Jesus Christ, becoming a Christian there is no need for delay. God is ready and willing to take you as his own right now.

You only have to ask him to forgive you and to give you help on the journey ahead which he will do by giving you the gift of the holy Spirit. It is a nurturing and personal partnership between God and yourself.

The act of deciding to change course in mid-life, is what is called conversion. You may also know it as being born again or deciding to be a Christian.

When you place your faith in Jesus, becoming utterly dependent upon him, you turn to God. That means that you have changed your intentions in the way you are going to live in future.

However, once you have made that decision, you leave behind your spiritual isolation and rebellion against him. As you live each day, becoming more involved with Jesus day by day, you will discover you are changing. You will find yourself doing things that please Jesus and developing your relationship with him.

You may well now be asking: "How is that relationship developed?" Until you enter a personal relationship with God, sin (all that which alienates you from God), controls your rebellion against him.

This sin is seen in your attitudes and your activities. God asks you to accept his management and guidance of your life. When you do that, God's point of view and his strength become your point of view and your source of strength. You turn your mind, will and heart to him for all you do.

If you want to become a Christian and start a new life of adventure following Jesus Christ, there are three simple steps to take:

Admit that you have done wrong against God and his ways and turn away from those attitudes.

Believe and trust in Jesus as your Saviour from the consequences of the anger of God towards you and your tendency to sin. Call on him, receive, trust, obey and worship him, recognizing him for who he is and what he has done.

Accept the holy Spirit of God into your life as the major motivating force for what you do. Once sin has been confessed, Jesus is believed in and trusted as Saviour then God the holy Spirit has entered your life, then you are a Christian.

All these things happen together instantly as you turn to God, being ready to grow in the grace and knowledge of Jesus! That is a WOW moment in your life. Welcome to the family of God. God has chosen you; Jesus has paid for you and has put his mark within you through the Holy Spirit (Ephesians 1:1-13).

Millions of people worldwide have done just that and are living proof of God's love for humanity. Why not join them?

Illustration Answers

Remember our Illustration Challenge? Here we go! Let's see how you did! Hope you thought outside the box for some of them – particularly if you thought of me and my own challenges as a cat!

1. Abandonment

2. Argument

3. Broken Heart

4. Confusion

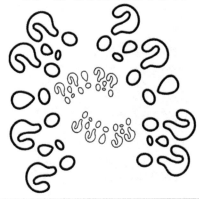

5. Death

6. Depression

7. Enemies

8. Failure

9. Fear

10. Guidance

11. Hunger

12. Lack Of Money

13. Loneliness

14. Peril

15. Persecution

16. Time:

17. Unemployment

18. Virus

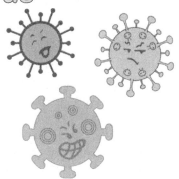

19. War

20. Work

About the Author

I was born in a small country town about 300 miles north east of Sydney in Australia. I was raised to be a sceptic cum agnostic cum atheist with the words "Churches are dangerous places" and this is like 30 years before Dawkins and his ilk uttered the words! So, coming into my teenage years in the eighties, I decided if they are so dangerous let's go for a bit of danger! So, I rebelled, became a Christian and started attending a local Christian youth group. After a bit, it was thought by my family that I was being brainwashed, so I was stopped from going for a couple of years, until I met somebody who I used to go to school with who invited me to her church, and I restarted from there...

As to how I came to the UK! Well, I came here from Australia for 6 months travel around Europe! Or so I thought! That was in 1990! I view it as God having a sense of humour. He knows I don't like rain, cold and in particular - together! He has even given me the most beautiful of women as a wife, but she doesn't like hot weather! God sure has a sense of humour! In 2003, I had a minor stroke and I view that as God giving me a clip round the ear to stop being stubborn and to listen to Him for direction. So instead of moving north with my job at Royal Mail, I took redundancy and went off to Moorlands college where I graduated in 2007.

I set up Partakers in 2007. I had recorded some audio files as part of a block placement during my 3rd year at Moorlands. Six months later I looked back on the site and discovered that the 16 audio files had been downloaded several thousand times, mainly in a country where evangelical Christians are persecuted. It was also part of my dissertation investigating if a Virtual Church could be part of the universal church. I based my study on the old maxim: one, holy, catholic and apostolic church.

I still took the normal route post-bible college and applied for pastor jobs around the UK. I often was interviewed but the 2 main reasons given for not being successful was that I was too radical (as in application and use of internet/digital space etc.), too much of a teacher or both! It was like "You can't seriously use the internet to evangelize and disciple others!" It was a bit like when the printing press came out and the church's collective bellybutton puckered and said, "You can't give the Bible to people, they may actually read it!"

So, I continued doing the Podcasts etc. To date Partakers Podcasting site has had about 1,500,000 unique visitors so far and about 4,000,000 downloads. The Partakers YouTube site has had over 1,500,000 viewings. I also have about 100 different contributors globally including several people from the church we are attached to and helping them to practice their gifting.

As for the name Partakers itself, I got the idea straight from Matthew 5:6, which I paraphrase as "Blessed are those who partake after righteousness for they will be filled."

I have an accountability team set up by the church we attend, for mentoring, prayer, guidance, advice and accountability. I also have people on Facebook & Twitter to keep an eye on what I say and do to see that those things are within biblical confines.

I currently reside in Bournemouth and travel frequently to speak in places including the UK USA and Australia. If you see fit, I would love to take the opportunity to visit you as well

Peace, blessings and jellybeans

Dave.

Dave G Roberts

Other Books By This Author

What's It All About Alphy? Series

What's It All About Alphy? The Lord's Prayer

ISBN: 978-1507801116

What's It All About, Alphy? Life Under Grace

ISBN: 978-1793020857

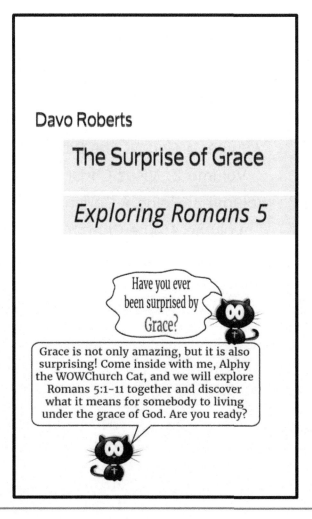

Glimpses Into Series:

Leviticus: A Book Of Joy

1 & 2 Chronicles: Books of Heritage and History

Psalms: A Book Of Life

Song Of Songs: A Book Of Relationship

Ezekiel: A Book Of Symbols And Visions

The Gospels: Books Of Good News

Acts: A Book Of Action

Romans: A Book Of Freedom

Read This Book Series:

Volume 1: God Of The Bible

Volume 2: Jesus Christ

Volume 3: Being A Christian

Volume 4: The Church

Volume 5: Evangelism

40 Days of Color: Coloring-In Devotional studies

AGOG: A Glimpse of God

An Ambassador in God's Orchestra of Joy

Dear Christian: Get A Good Grip

Dear Church: Wake up! Issues for the Church today

Developing Intimacy With God

Easter Essentials: Exploring Easter

Exploring The Bible:

God Gets His Hands Dirty

God, Internet Church & You

God's Two Words For You: Straight talk about Jesus and the Bible

Helping the Forgotten Church

Heroes And Heretics Abound: The Making of the Modern Church

Intimacy with God

Living Life Right: Studies in Romans 12

Scriptural Delights: Exploring Psalm 119

The Surprise of Grace: Alphy Looks Into Romans 5

When Love Hits Town: The New Testament Story

WOW Disciple Book 02: Living Life

WOW Words of the Bible

All books are available in Paperback and Kindle at:

PulpTheology.co.uk

PulpTheology.com

And all Amazon sites

About Partakers

Vision Statement: Partakers exists to communicate and disseminate resources for the purposes of Christian Discipleship, Evangelism and Worship by employing radical and relevant methods, including virtual reality and online distribution.

Mission Statement: Helping the world, one person at a time, to engage in whole life discipleship, as Partakers of Jesus Christ.

info@partakers.co.uk

www.partakers.co.uk

Printed in Great Britain
by Amazon

38105078R10086